I Haven't Lived At All

Evelyn Knightley

I HAVEN'T LIVED AT ALL

Copyright © 2013 Evelyn Knightley

All rights reserved. This book or any portion thereof may not be reproduced or used in any manner whatsoever without the express written permission of the publisher except for the use of brief quotations in a book review.

Printed in the United Kingdom

First Printing, 2013

ISBN-10: 0957682301
ISBN-13: 978-0957682306

Cover Art © Yasmin Matthews

Edited by Cynthia Shepp

Constellation Publishing Ltd

Oxford, UK

TO ALL OF YOU;
PAST, PRESENT AND FUTURE.

CONTENTS

POETRY

On The Moon - 1
Beat - 2
The Haunted - 3
You Let Go – 4
Digits – 5
Liberty - 6
Dreaming – 8
Paper Screams – 9
I Know Nothing At All – 10
Over – 11
Inhale – 12
The City – 13
Backseat - 14
It's Not – 15
The Water Gets Deeper – 16
You Don't Want To Be Saved – 17
Memories of a Time – 18
Your Creation – 20
Scripted – 21
The Clown – 22
Know – 23
I'll Make It Worth The Wait – 24
Twenty-One – 25

SHORT STORIES

Shattered – 27
Work In Progress – 33
Fractured Fantasy – 37
Ending Seasons – 42
Death – 45

*

About the Author – 48
Disconnected – 50
Soundtrack -57

ACKNOWLEDGMENTS

This has been a rather self-indulgent pursuit, and throughout the process of creating and compiling this collection that has become increasingly clear to me.
The idea for "I Haven't Lived At All" threw itself at me whilst I was in the process of deciding if University was the right choice for me. Two years into my course, it still wasn't sitting right with me and I could never quite figure out why. As it happens, all of my questioning really was pointless. I realised I was spending less time focusing on assignments, I really had no interest in a career in Psychology, and a lot more time procrastinating and feeling like I was missing out on something spectacular in life. I became incredibly sick of saying, "Well, I study Psychology, but in an ideal world I've always wanted to write." I had to give myself a metaphorical slap around the face, because of course the world is never ideal for anybody and nothing was ever going to happen for me simply because that was a sentence I had used over many years. To put it bluntly, I felt trapped, and I was my own prison. So I made the choice to leave University for a world of working full-time (in a job I less than love) and instead indulged in the idea of creating my own collection of work and getting it out there for people to read. As I'm sat writing this in the sun, with my alabaster skin slowly burning, I now realise that this whole process feels incredibly natural.

Sometimes I have to remind myself that I really haven't lived at all, and whilst I may have reasons to feel bad or bitter about the world or things that have happened in my life, there's a lot more out there and it's up to me to go searching for it. Living shouldn't be about focusing on the bad, but having faith in the good. I've had to learn a lot along the way, both about myself and about the business side of publishing a book. This is something I'm sure will be a never-ending process and that's something I'm completely happy to accept. Strangely, I've had to learn to accept the kindness of others, and I'm still not entirely at ease with this, but the support keeps on coming and proves my doubts wrong each and every time. This is where I say thank you and I can never say it enough, especially to those of you who supported this book during the Kickstarter stage. You've overwhelmed me with your kindness and faith in me. This book has only been possible because of you and for this I will be forever grateful.

Kickstarter Dedication

Liam Binns. Tom Buckle. Jozefine Cox. Charlotte Emma Curtis. Wendy Dant. Hannah Endacott. Jonas De Keukelaere. Emma Drinkwater and Gareth Franklin. Kim Häggblom. Helen Harper. Ilythia Harte. Ella Hicks. Natalie, Lynda and Jud Hind. Adhiya Jawed. Francesca Jayawardena. Joseph Lauzier. Luke Maycock. Sarah Mason. Victoria O'Rourke. Léyla Richardson. Lynda Simms. Charlotte Simms. Carl Twynham. Amy Webb.

I would also like to give a special thanks to Yasmin Matthews for creating the cover art for this book and for many other aspects of this project, and to Victoria O'Rourke for helping me with this entire process; be it with editing, formatting or just being on the receiving end of my nonsensical, sleep deprived, and coffee fueled emails.

ON THE MOON

I lived on the moon
and I would look down and watch you.
I used to wonder if you knew I was there.

I lived on the moon
and I wanted to play with you.
I used to wonder if you knew I was there.

I lived on the moon
and it was always cold and dark.
I used to wonder if you knew I was there.

I lived on the moon
and I wished I could be elsewhere.
I used to wonder if you knew I was there.

BEAT

The beat of your heart
is all that you have and it's
beating its way out.

THE HAUNTED

Silence,
hold your breath.

Silently,
they're coming for you.

And when they try to take you away,
don't be afraid to follow them.
As they reach out their hands,
your heart leaps to your throat,
and you feel them pull you
towards one path
or another.

So you reach out your hand,
and your skin begins to freeze.
You feel it all flooding back
into your mind,
breaking down.

YOU LET GO

I looked you in the eye
and the rain fell down on my face.
I held your hands and told you
I loved you.
You let go.
I never did.

DIGITS

I stare at the digits:
on the clock,
at the cash point,
on the scales,
on the packaging,
on the screen.

I wonder when the numbers became important,
when they gained control of my life.
I wonder when maths became my strong point,
when it gained control of my life.

LIBERTY

I love
the way you stand alone,
the way you stand against the storm.

And I remember,
when I was small,
I would dream of standing with you.

You always looked
so safe and strong,
so I longed to be alongside you.

As I grew up,
I kept you in my mind,
measuring myself against you;

thinking about how the storm still touched me.

One day,
I decided I wanted to know
what kept you alive.

You are made of copper
and steel.
This keeps you alive

and you cannot feel.

Over the years,
we saw you change.
Changed by the world.

Still,
you were standing
and you stood strong.

I looked at myself,
a cobweb of nerves
coated by skin.

This was my protection,
but still, I can feel.
I could never withstand the storm.

I think
that though we're made of differences,
we are both man-made.

Made to withstand
the ones that could ruin us;
the people that created us.

We are symbols,
of guidance,
of protection.

That is something
that has since been forgotten
and many things stand to harm us.

Now,
I worry.
I tried to stand the way you did.

Alone and strong.
I admired that,
but I couldn't do it for very long.

DREAMING

Take me to a place
where sugar-coated dreams come true.
I'll stay in a world of make-believe.

PAPER SCREAMS

When I was a child,
I would cry,
and no one ever heard me.
So I would scream
and no one ever heard me.

It's much like that today,
but sometimes being silent
is a lot like being dead.
So my body fights out
with these paper screams.
Stained and creased
and carved with ink.

These paper screams are silent too,
because no one ever heard me.

I KNOW NOTHING AT ALL

Thirteen was when I knew it all,
that it was my time to go.
It was the time words founds me
and I stopped searching for anything.
I claimed the night as my home
and announced my heart was broken.

Thirteen was when I lost the war,
threw my bullet-less gun down.
It was the time sharpness found me
and I found my greatest friend.
I claimed the sorrow as my home
and announced my life as over.

Thirteen was when I knew nothing at all,
and I gave up far too soon.
It was the time when I let you win,
and gave you more than I should.
I claimed despair as my own
and announced that this was it.

OVER

It was my last smile, and it was weak.
I opened my mouth; I could not speak.
It had been a long fight to get this far
and now, I was ready to raise the flag.
I closed my eyes for the last time
and I did not feel sad.
All of you flooded over me
and I was numb.

I waited.
Over,
red rover, red rover.
Over and out

I told myself.
Over,
red rover, red rover.
Over and out.

Morning came anyway,
and still I was numb.

INHALE

I told you I wanted to kill myself,
and you didn't say a word.
I watched you
inhale
exhale
cigarette smoke.
I told you that there's nothing left,
nothing worth fighting for.
I watched you
inhale
exhale

inhale.

You looked at me,
holding me in your stare.
You fight for you,
that is all you're meant to do.
It's a fight worth fighting.

I slipped away.

THE CITY

I was thinking of the city,
of the nights I spent alone.
The world was rushing beneath me,
                        and I was alone.

BACKSEAT

I was always on the backseat of your car,
in the backseat of your life,
no seatbelt, no safety.
I was ready and waiting
for the collision,
for the explosion.

I didn't have to wait long.

IT'S NOT

It's not that I want to see you burn
and it's not that I would harm you,
but if I were to see you on the floor
crying out for mercy—
I would turn the other way.

It's not that I hate you
and it's not that I think of you,
but if you were to crawl to my feet
crying to be saved—
I would turn the other way.

It's not that I hold any ill feelings
and it's not that I have erased you,
but when I cried in your arms
and begged you not to leave me—
You turned the other way.

THE WATER GETS DEEPER

How did it become this?
Dreams spoken and then broken,
Lies left wide open.

I tried to create a new world,
where darkness is banned.
Where it could be me and you—
you could save me and I would love you.

Surrounded by conspiracies,
and showered by hate,
I wait for you, yet I stand alone.

I have burned cities down,
fighting to get to this, to you.
And now I stand here,
in this wasteland I created.
Still I search for you.

This was never the way I thought it would be,
with my heart in the sky,
and my head on the floor.

YOU DON'T WANT TO BE SAVED

That day, when you looked away.
That day, when you walked away.

I don't know if you had given up.
I don't know if you want to start again.

I still think of you, and who you might be,
I still think of you, of you with me.

I can only tell you that I tried,
I really tried to save you.
I think, somewhere
along
the
line

you died.

MEMORIES OF A TIME

If I look down to the times that have passed,
I can see the faint light of something small.
I try to reach out, to feel the lightness on my fingertips.
It all seems so far away and I can't stretch out far enough.
I can hear the sound of the lives that have come and gone.
I can hear the sound of a tiny heart beat, so distant, so clouded.
There are some things I can touch.
There are some things I can taste.
I can taste the fear; the hatred that's shadowing the light.
I can see a photograph, of smiles and happiness,
of lies and tales of untold truths.

And I can see a room, decorated so brightly,
so naïvely.
There are pictures and books and paintings.
I can see a life that's decorated too.
There is a spark flickering beneath it all, trying to grow brighter,
trying to signal to the world outside.

Outside of the room where everything seems bright,
there's a blackness surrounding the flickering spark,
the dimming light.
Outside of the room, everything is darker,
the photographs of smiles are long forgotten
and all that's left are broken bones and broken hearts.

Still, I can see the light, fainter than ever,
trying to shine brighter, trying to fight out the blackness.
Trying to fix the broken bones, trying to fix the broken hearts.
But in the memories of times that have passed,
there's only one light. And there's a blanket of darkness,
and it's suffocating and it's destroying.
I look, and I can see that it is fading away,
and all of the hatred and the lies and the tears are winning.
The light is still dimming.

I can hear the sound of lives that are still present,
of the evilness that is still growing.
The sound isn't so muffled anymore, and the darkness has won.
But the sound is blasting at me, the speakers set on full volume.
The photographs become moving images,
from the smiles to the frowns to the tears and to the hurt.
The picture speeds up and years are flashing in front of my eyes,
and all the colour has been drained, replaced by black and grey.
The people in these pictures come and go.
They fight and they leave destruction in their path.

I look deeper and I can feel the powerless light.
It's in the back of the moving images, just watching,
and never touching the lives that lay before it.
Everything is so untouchable,
everything is so strong

and the light is so weak.

Still, the images move faster,
moving towards me and never seeming to slow to a halt.
I blink, and I open my eyes,
this time it's all moving around me.

Sometimes, the memories of times that have passed
are instead the memories of times that are present.
This time, I look, and I can see.
There's not a single bit of lightness,
just a girl, and a life, and people, and their lives,
and the memories of times that have passed.

YOUR CREATION

This face.
This face that I confuse for yours.
On the wall,
in the mirror,
this face was always yours.

Your touch.
Your touch that killed me,
In the night,
in my sleep,
your touch was always mine.

Our secret.
Our secret that keeps us together,
You and I,
just us two,
our secret is always mine.

My life.
My life that you ended,
in my nightmares,
in my waking hours,
my life was always yours.

SCRIPTED

It took a second to build these walls.
Even longer to fight,
to keep it all out:
the laughter, the faces,
the disguises.

Don't be fooled by the lights.
The world takes the role of villain,
"Keep your enemies close," too close.

Locks and chains,
ironmongery in your veins.

"All the world is a stage,"
and it's your curtain call.
Take your place at centre stage,
lights shining down and reflecting on your skin.
Burning into your soul.
Exposing.
Never quite enough.

                               A smile—Act 1, scene 1.

THE CLOWN

Ten years ago, I went to the circus
and I sat and we all laughed.
Everybody gasped together,
held hands together,
laughed together.
The men with the bodies two feet shorter than I
walked in and they laughed too.
We all cheered as they somersaulted through the air,
with our eyes transfixed on their every move.
I only once turned my attention away,
to say thank you to the man who handed me popcorn.

A toy car was in the middle,
and out climbed fifteen men
with their faces painted white.
They threw things at each other
and pretended to cry when it was meant to hurt.
We all laughed,
and they laughed too.

It was a good day,
and I was carried to the car,
feeling tired and sick from candy floss.
I still look back and laugh about that day,
but now I think,
that's the world we live in.

KNOW

Know that you will be okay.
Know that you're not alone.
Know that there is a tomorrow,
and if that day is unkind
there will be another;
it will come without the sorrow.

Know that it's okay to crumble.
Know that you're never too broken.
Know that you've healed before.
Each morning you wake
there will be a new chance
to grow that little bit more.

Know that wounds can heal.
Know that it's never too late.
Know that each time you fall,
and each time you hit the bottom,
you'll never learn to walk
if at first you don't learn to crawl.

Know that I'm beside you.
Know that I fall too.
Know that in the darkest nights,
and in the shadow of the days,
I feel what you feel too.
I'm here to fight your fights.

Know that you will be okay.
Know that you're not alone.
We will stand together
and we'll be waiting for the dawn.

I'LL MAKE IT WORTH THE WAIT

I'll make it worth the wait, she said,
with her eyes glazed
and her fists clenched.
A bold statement, I thought,
but I knew what she meant.
Because when you think of all the hours,
all the days and all the time you waste,
doing nothing or feeling sorry,
something has to make you carry on;
waking up and going to sleep.
I think we're all waiting for something, she said,
I'm just saying I'll make it worth the wait.

TWENTY-ONE

I was twenty when I thought I was done
but now I'm twenty-one,
and there are twenty-one things
I still want to do
and twenty-one people
I still want to be.
I think I'm just getting started.

SHATTERED

She walked along the dimly lit corridor, occasionally stopping to listen for any movements coming from elsewhere. She could just about make out the shape of each thick frame on the wall, hanging from a rusty nail and obscured by dust that had settled. Walking along, she traced her finger across the embossed wallpaper, only allowing her finger to leave its path if a hole or crack tried to consume it. She made her hand leap across the doorway, recognising the correct moment to break contact and then changing her thoughts from the doors to the mildew-laden window far ahead.

The night carried the same recognisable obscurity as it had the previous night, and the many nights before that. The usual whisperings would play repetitively in her mind—uttering words that she could not quite understand. They tormented her each and every night and yet they remained just as unclear as they always had been. It was just a part of the way things were, the way things had been for as long as she could remember; the way things were always going to be. She couldn't tell you how old she was, or the colour of her hair, or how long she'd been there and how aged her face would now be. Identity had become unimportant, a forgotten and distant concept.

What she would describe as many years ago, she had decided to break contact with herself. She fought to break from her body, her prison, in a bid to leave this world behind. The whisperings overwhelmed her one night, so she threw her fist into the only mirror in the house. She walked away from the room and had never returned since. She had left scattered shards of mirror on the floor, and that satisfied her. The importance of a mirror is to show a reflection—with no reflection she had no identity and therefore no importance or responsibilities. Her lack of identity became unimportant and irrelevant. While the sun began to rise, much the same as always, dew drops scurried down the windows as the new light attempted to warm the frozen droplets. Beads of light slowly started pouring in, highlighting the grains of dirt that had become cemented to the young girl's petticoat over the years. That day would be spent like all the rest were. She would gaze out of the window, trying to piece together the small bits of detail of the outside world, which she could gather in each clean streak on the glass. She would daydream and wonder, and she would sit and try to forget that she was trying to remember something. She had an obsession with trying to find her way to a place called home, yet this corridor was the only place she knew. It was a cycle she experienced each and every day, and for each day she continued to be alone, she would grow increasingly separated from life. No matter how hard she fought to escape from the walls that had imprisoned her, they were unrelenting and as she grew weaker, they grew closer to her.

Another day had disappeared, and the dark sky cloaked over the house, as though adding an extra security measure in order to ensure she would not escape. As she walked around aimlessly, stroking each indent along the cold, harsh walls, the only company she had that night was the sound of the trees tauntingly scratching the outside of the windows, reminding her that an outside existed.

As she reached yet another dead end in the dark labyrinth of a house, she sank against the wall as she felt her energy beginning to decrease—more so than ever before. She placed her hand around her neck and reached for the only sense of recognition she had ever felt any empathy for. A small silver necklace hung loosely from her neck. As she traced the outline of the delicate trinket, she hovered as she could feel the same recognisable confusion rush through her; the same confusion that would happen every time she felt out the letter "L" and could once again not remember what the "L" stood for. Another part of her long forgotten memory, but she treasured this piece. It had become the one thing in her life that she had grown to love.

The wind died down and the shadows of troubled souls that had been chasing each other against the walls decided it was time to rest once again. There would be another chance for them to be reunited again the next night. As she prepared herself to face the rest of the night alone in the threatening cold that the house carried, giggling began filling the house. It was distant and sounded as though it had been transmitted through an old radio, as distant as it sounded, she could not help but feel as though the noise was made for her. For the first time, she felt this noise was not meant to taunt her, instead it was meant to call her home.

She tried to ignore it for a while, but her thoughts kept flickering back to her longing for the feeling of innocence; the desire to have the sun beaming down on her face. She longed to feel that little bit more alive. Over time, she had learned that if she closed her eyes for long enough, and focused hard enough, she could vaguely smell the freshly cut grass seasoned with the floral scent of Orchids. She could feel the wind tap against her skin and feel the warmth upon her arms. Yet she did not know how she could imagine this, when all she had known was the darkness of the walls that swallowed her.

Many rooms had been left unopened and cobwebs had started taking over many of the hidden corners and corridors. Many nights had been and gone since she had heard that small glimmer of life, of hope, and after many arguments with herself, she decided to promise that she would begin to explore again. She would try to find her way out, to wherever she was supposed to be. She had grown certain that, despite everything she had ever believed, this was not where she was destined to belong. She began a slow walk to the west of the house, and she tightly held on to the necklace for a sense of comfort. When she reached the furthest set of stairs, she looked up at an old door surrounded by beams of light shining out through the cracks. This was a place she had never visited before, and she couldn't shake her discomfort with this fact; for she was sure that she had been to every corner of the house many times before. Despite this, she trusted the sense of hope she had experienced, and took the long journey up to the door. Each stair she stood on let a groan out, complaining of old age and negligence. The door handle was cold and metal flaked away as she placed her hand on it, but it opened with ease. Behind the door was a world that seemed so different from the rest of the house, as though it didn't belong there. The pale purple paint work was still pristine and the thick cream carpet looked as though it was untouched. A bed was placed up against the back wall and on it was carefully placed bedding and stuffed toys that had not been played with. Net curtain had been hung in the window, and they showed the only signs of neglect as they had turned a faded yellow and were most likely the cause of a slight musty smell that danced about the room as soon as the door had been opened.

She closed the door behind her and placed herself on the bed, being careful not to crease the sheets. As she sat silently, slow tears started to trace down her cheeks. An overwhelming feeling of happiness and warmth flooded over her. She recognised this room. She had an instant fondness for the large bear with a maroon scarf that seemed to be looking at her from the end of the bed. She allowed herself a few moments to experience the new-ness of the warmth, of comfort, of recognition. She began to touch the sheets around her in a bid to confirm to herself that she was located where she believed herself to be. Her hand touched a pillow and she felt something hard resting underneath it. She gently lifted a corner of the pillow up, being careful not to disturb her surroundings too greatly. From underneath the pillow, she lifted out a thick notebook. It was of a light pink colour and covered in tiny gems so it sparkled as the sun hit it. As she held her hands on it, she felt what she had longed to feel for so long—her identity.

    She opened up the first page and it was as though she had opened her eyes for the first time ever. Written across the front page, in small, curled handwriting, was, "My name is Lórien Hawley. I am nine years old and I live with my mummy, my daddy, and my little brother. I like reading and writing and I also like going out for walks with my mum. She sometimes lets me play in the brook, as long as I'm careful not to fall over any stones." Next to this was a small black and white photo. Though faded, she could still make out a pretty young girl, with long, dark hair and fair skin. Standing behind her was a young man, a woman, and a small boy who looked identical to the girl. A happy family, like she had always dreamed of. On the back of the photo was written, "The Hawley's—September 17th 1876".

    Over the next pages were many messages, all in different handwriting with dates underneath them.

    "Mummy loves you, darling. I'm so sorry. Please don't be afraid. We'll all see you soon. – September 19th 1876."
"I miss you and I miss playing with you. Love you, Mark –

September 19th 1876"
"We never could keep you away from that place. Don't worry, sweetheart, you won't be alone. Grandma will be waiting for you. Love you with my entire heart –

Daddy. September 19th 1876."
"Lórien, I always told you that you shouldn't play around in the brook without me. I'm going to miss you. Don't forget me. I won't forget you! Love Isabel – October 2nd 1876."

    She placed the book back down without reading any further. As she walked over to the mirror for the first time in a long time, tears continued to fall down her cheeks. Looking into the mirror she could see no reflection, and she remembered why she had been so angered last time. She had felt that she was being deceived, but this time she felt different. She knew who she was, even without her reflection. She turned to take a further look around the room, remembering that she had once loved a doll with curly blonde hair. As she turned, she heard voices, and in front of her she saw the same people that she had seen in the photograph moments before. She looked into their eyes, and the warmth she had always longed for flooded her body. They reached out their arms and pulled her into an embrace. It was then that she knew who, and where, she was.

    She was Lórien Hawley, aged nine, and she died doing what she loved most. She never knew it, but she had always been home.

WORK IN PROGRESS

11.30 PM. Almost time to go home. I could feel a blister breaking out on the back of my ankle; it was my body's way of punishing me for wearing shoes two sizes too small for me for eight hours straight. I kept propping myself up against the bar, in the hope that my feet could grab a ten-second break. I contemplated removing my shoes completely, and then I thought of what substances have fallen on this floor—the idea wasn't that appealing after that.

It was a Wednesday night—darts night. Since being here, I had learnt that if you took enough time to look at all the faces of the people in here, you could begin to learn how the village worked. I had discovered that this pub acted as a model village for the real thing. At the far end of the bar, you could see a small group of men between thirty and fifty, all drinking pints of Stella and only occasionally leaving their stool when they stepped out to the pub garden to light up a cigarette. (This was a ritual that was not made complete without a five-minute rant about the smoking ban—double this length of time during the winter months.)

The rest of the population of the pub was made up with your typical countryside-type men complete with their flat caps and pipes, and their wives all congregating around a table. They would sit with their small glasses of dry white wine, discussing the day's events and the latest gossip that had made its trip around the village. Their husbands stood scattered across the length of the bar, with various drinks spread out in front of them. Their conversations were always hardest to keep up with; it would vary from sport, to work, then crude joke time, a long complaining session about their wives nagging, and then it would make its way back to sport again. All of this could be going on simultaneously and I had just learned when the correct time to laugh or nod my head was. I tried to avoid joining their conversations as much as possible as every topic of interest went over my head.

As bored as I got doing the same things every day, I had once grown to love this job. Every so often the daily grind would be interrupted by the odd, drunken argument, but other than those rare times, everybody was always friendly to one another. This was why I had left home to begin with. I had always enjoyed learning new things, not the nonsense school teaches you, but studying people had become a hobby of mine. I felt by watching others, I could learn everything I needed to. It was never that easy though, as systematic as the days in The King's Heart became, I could never quite make out what each person was about. It was only when a stranger entered the pub on their own that I could really gain any insight as to who they were, and why they were there.

Humans, I had decided, were fascinatingly perplexing.

The mind can think of many things in a short amount of time, I discovered. Whilst I had been analysing the human population of The King's Heart, I had failed to notice how slowly the hands were wandering around the face of the clock.
There was only so much I could entertain myself with. I had been working in the same place for over eight months. That doesn't seem like a very long time, but I was impatient and never stayed in the same place long enough to become bored of it—impatient and ambitious I suppose you could call me. There was nothing to achieve from working behind a bar, and once all the locals knew your name there was nothing else to strive towards. All of my hopes I had for the future seemed to go forgotten whilst I stood in the same place. I couldn't help but feel trapped.

11.42 PM, time still against me—another round of dry white wine was needed.

"One last round for our better halves, please love," was detected with my built-in pub radar.

"Coming up, Roy," said with my fake yet pleasant smile plastered on. I was never very happy when my daydreams were interrupted. Unfortunately, it seemed to be happening more and more often.

"Last round mind you, if I have to put up with Anne's snoring again, I won't be held responsible for the actions I may take."

I laughed, "You old charmer, Roy. Irresistible to the best of us, isn't that right?" Friendly pub banter, it had become a skill of mine. Like most locals in this little village, he had a jolly smile that would remind you of St. Nicholas, just not as generous. He was more of a Granddad figure that you could imagine boring you with stories of "When I was a young lad..."

All drinks served up, that was another five minutes I had managed to kill. I wouldn't say I hated this job now—at least I tried not to. I tried my hardest to see it as a red traffic light that had become frozen and I was just another car it was holding back. That thought did not stop the frustration that everybody feels during a traffic jam.

Since working at the pub, each day seemed to be a copy of the previous day. Wake up, jump into the shower to wash my hair, discover I was running late as usual, shove on my makeup, and pull my hair up into a pathetic excuse for a ponytail—followed by a streak of energy that allowed me to run out of the front door. My energy never lasted long as far as work was concerned, so I would spend the rest of the journey searching for motivation to drag each foot in front of the other.

From there, I would spend the rest of my waking hours dreaming about what could be—if I could just get out. At the end of it, the bar was where I ended up. The same old bar, serving the same old people.

FRACTURED FANTASY

Once upon a time there was a small town nestled between permanently golden fields. There was nothing else to be found within a five-mile radius—it was a town that thrived in its isolation. Amongst this nothingness, a tall townhouse stood out. It was odd for many reasons. Whilst the location itself added an air of mystery, the building itself was unkempt and the garden surrounding it grew wilder by the year. The small family that lived inside were equally as solitary and little was known about them. Few in the town knew of their names; none knew their faces. It was rumored that the house belonged to a mother and her daughter. The only sight of life that could be spotted was the face of a young girl peering out of the window as the sun set. No one knew her age; no one had dared venture close enough to identify any aspect of her. It was thought by those who lived in the town that there was something a little queer about a family that never seemed to leave the house—and even more so about a family that consisted of only females. No man had ever been seen approaching the house. In fact, many feared being in the presence of the building and would often choose an alternative route so they could avoid it.

Whilst the outside of the house appeared to be neglected, the inside told a much different story. Everything was pristine, everything was minimal. There were no photographs, the only electricity used was for kitchen appliances and lighting, and the floor was made of solid wood and looked as though it was religiously polished. As for the habitants, they too were equally as pristine. The mother had long, curly hair and dressed simply in a long, flowing skirt and long-sleeved T-shirt. Whilst the daughter, Adrianna, was clothed in simple white dresses and seldom wore shoes.

It was clear to see by her face that the mother had been badly hurt in the past. Her face itself did not appear to be aged, but there was a sadness in her eyes that never left and a harshness to her face that never lifted. As such, she had chosen to spend the rest of her life in solitude. She tried to instill this way of living into her Adrianna, reminding her that whilst she may feel lonely, it was only to protect her from being hurt. As Adrianna grew older, the tale of her mother's woes was told more and more frequently. A tale of how she once loved a man, and a tale of how he almost killed her and Adrianna. At first, he appeared to be the man of her dreams. He would soon learn her secrets and was unwilling to accept her as she was. Underneath his smile, a cruel man was waiting to be unleashed and he relished in the opportunity she gave him. He saw her as undeserving of life, and so he took it into his own hands to rid her of it.

Though Adrianna was reminded of this, she couldn't comprehend a world in which all people would react the way her father did. She tried to understand her mother, and she tried to respect her rules, but she could not rid herself of the dreams she was frequented by; the dreams of her life being full of laughter and love, not secrecy and lies. These dreams had been fueled by the books she kept inside her bedroom, from old fairytales to modern romance stories. She had read horror stories too, but they sounded much too like her mother, so she had decided not to keep those. She absorbed all of these stories and they would swim around her mind, consuming her every thought. She longed to make these stories come true. She wanted to live her own fairytale.

She felt as though she should be special, but she could never explain why. Her mother had yet to explain to her, but on her eighteenth birthday, she would learn that it was possible for her dreams to come true. She was indeed very special, and she possessed a gift others could only dream of. As soon as she turned eighteen, she would have the power to turn her wishes into reality, but her mother knew that it couldn't be as simple as that. There was a risk that though her dreams would come true—so too may her fears. Adrianna, unaware of this, spent every night looking outside of her bedroom window, wondering what it was her mother was keeping her from. She wanted to experience the world.

*

On the eve of Adrianna's eighteenth birthday, she felt much the same as always, only this time she was aware that the next day would bring the chance of freedom. She loved her mother, but as she had grown older, she had become detached from her and her desire to leave the house grew stronger. As an adult, she hoped her mother would respect this decision. It scared her, as she hated the thought of hurting her mother, but as she re-read the fairytales that had followed her through her life, she knew that the path of freedom was the path for her.

As she sat in, gazing out of the window just like any other night, her mother tapped quietly on her bedroom door before entering. She greeted her with a soft kiss on her head. It was this night that Adrianna learnt of her gifts, and of her mother's fear. Her heart was too bold to be stopped by fear; it yearned for adventure, for friendship, for love. Nothing, not even her mother's threats, could stop her. The next day, before the sun had risen, she quietly left the house and set out on what she would call the first day of her life. With nothing but the knowledge and confirmation of her gift, she never looked back—the road was her home.

She had no plans as to where she would like to end up, and in that moment she found herself in a state of bliss. She could hear the birds awakening; the sound of their chirps no longer blocked by a glass window. That was her first connection with the world, the birds. She sat at the roadside, listening to their morning chorus and wished that they would greet her into the world—just like she had read in the fairytales.

Within seconds, a flock of birds surrounded her, chirping and taking small, cautious steps closer. They gathered around her feet, and she leant down to slightly stroke them with her fingers. She found herself talking to them as though they were long lost friends. Moments later, her newfound friendship was interrupted by the sound of a car approaching quickly. In the distance, she could see a large red car approaching. As it grew closer, it began to slow down before coming to a halt alongside.

Inside, an elderly lady sat. She rolled down her window and peered out at the girl sat on the roadside. Adrianna rose to her feet, at first cautiously, until she had an idea. "I wish that this old lady would take me to the nearest town." As though the old lady had read her mind, she was invited into the car and back to the old lady's home for breakfast.

Adrianna sat in the car for what felt like hours, at first she was too shy to speak, but she soon grew confidence as she remembered that her wishes come true. As far as she was aware, absolutely nothing could go wrong.

*

As they approached the old lady's house, Adrianna's mind darted back to her mother at home. She would have been awake by now, frantic out of her mind with worry. Adrianna began to doubt if she was right to leave her home far behind and put trust into the kindness of strangers.

It wasn't long until her worries became reality.

Unaware that her mother had missed out one crucial detail, as her fears became stronger, so too did the old lady. There was no sign of breakfast, instead Adrianna was pushed into the basement and the door was locked tightly. She tried crying and shouting, but she knew no one could hear her. As the night drew closer, she became more tired and ceased crying. That night, her dreams were tormented. She held on to the thought of love, yet she could not rid herself of the cruelty she had experienced.

She was awoken by a loud bang. She looked up to see the door to the basement had been broken open and a dark figure was approaching her. She could tell that it was not the old lady, as this figure was much taller and much broader. As the figure grew closer, she could make out the detail of its face. A handsome man, with a strong jaw and what she guessed were icy blue eyes knelt down at her side. It was the moment she had dreamt of. She felt the connection instantly; it was magnetic. She put her hand to his face and he pulled her closely to him in an embrace. Happiness flooded her body.

It was then that a flashback from a dream entered her mind. She remembered a story in which a wife was killed by her husband. She remembered that the same had almost happened to her mother.

It was then that she felt it—a piercing blow to her stomach. She gently touched her stomach and felt blood oozing out of her. She glanced up into the eyes of this stranger, his eyes now black. He smirked and backed away towards the door. Her eyes grew heavy and the room around her began to spin. She thought back to her mother and all of the fights they had. She wished she could be back home.

As she slipped in and out of consciousness, her eyes flickered open one last time. She saw her mother's tearful face gazing down at her and felt her arms wrap around her. With her last bit of strength, Adrianna whispered, "I'm sorry. I only wanted my happily ever after."

A dark shadow cast over her mother's face as a smile formed and she replied, "Darling, fairytales were never real." She let out a quiet cackle and laid Adrianna back on to the floor.

She was right, Adrianna thought, *this wasn't at all how her fantasy was meant to end*

ENDING SEASONS

I don't like today.

Everything about it is weird. I opened my eyes and all I could see was yellow. Everything looks hazy; I don't think I can feel where my hands are. I don't know if I can feel them attached to my body. I don't know if I could ever feel it but the fact that I'm no longer able to fills me with unease. I looked outside, and it wasn't yellow there. It wasn't the weather. I'd hoped to gain some sense of pathetic fallacy to explain this 'yellow-ness'. There was wind, (my state of mind: unpredictable? Naturally.), and it was cloudy (depressed? No shit.). There was no yellow out there, no sun to blame for this. The clouds invaded the off-blue colour of the sky, and the strong wind was busy unsettling the branches of the trees. Autumn was long gone, and so too were the autumnal colours that I would have hoped to see in order to explain this situation I found myself in. I didn't like this feeling. I didn't recognise it. I felt that someone had tipped a small splash of dye into my world, invaded it without my permission. I didn't like it. It wasn't welcome.

The yellow was just the start of it all. It made me want to crawl back to bed and shield myself with my duvet. For a few moments I questioned if I was still alive, if I was dreaming, if this was me slipping into insanity—something I had suspected would happen long ago. I was torn between the need to escape the touch of the yellow, the obligation to attend the first lecture of the new term, and the fear that once I opened my bedroom door the world would be completely different. That everything I believed to be real was a lie—and always had been.

I think I must have stood staring out of the window for an abnormally long amount of time. My inner debate was interrupted by a violent banging on the door.

"Are you coming or not?"

Messy and fast, my thoughts battled against each other to find the places where they should be. It was early, and I'd been confused from the moment I woke up.

Bang. Bang. Bang.

I needed to locate that voice, I recognised it and it was just a matter of elimination. My mind was just preoccupied...with the yellow, and the wind. But not the sun, because there was no sun. There never is. Everything was already out of sync. Everything already felt distant and whilst this voice knew of my existence, I wasn't entirely convinced of it.

It wasn't Deb, she never banged the door. It wasn't in her nature. She never shouted, either. She was the silent one. It wasn't Deb. I know Hannah isn't in my class this morning; she's not in any class that would mean it was necessary for her to be up before noon. It was a female voice, so it wasn't Dan or Kyle.

"Jen…Jenny…Jennifer? We are going to be late!" My door shook in response to her voice.

It hit me, it was Kate. Besides the fact that she was the only one I had yet to erase from my mental list, she's also the only one who has the ability to make the windows rattle when she shouts.

I began to pull myself away from the window. I hadn't forgotten the yellow, and I doubted if I ever could. Still, this meant I had to try; I had to try to reconnect with wherever I am…whoever I am. I would go to my lecture and I would see that the sky today is blue-grey, and the trees are brown and golden, the grass is green and so are my eyes. My hair is brown, like the trees. There isn't a single bit of yellow, not really.

I walked over to the door, hair unkempt.

"Coming… I'm coming. I—I was…sleeping."

I opened the door slightly and peeked out. Kate stood there with one arm ready to bang on the door again, the other balancing a pile of books with a travel mug carefully lodged on top.

"Christ, hibernating were you? Hurry up, you've got ten minutes or I'm leaving and you'll have to walk there." She sped off down the hall, kicking the doors open with her feet before letting in a gust of wind as she entered the world where things aren't yellow.

I hurried to get dressed. My mind had cleared itself up as it yearned for the outside. The yellow was becoming suffocating, so I needed to be on the other side of the window and I would never look back through to this side.

Yellow. *It's all yellow in here*, I thought to myself.

I opened the window and felt the wind on my face for the last time. I looked down, and saw the only thing that hadn't been tainted, and I knew I could escape.

No. I can't say I'm at all fond of yellow.

DEATH

The world had ended and they were alone.

The scene before them was something that could only be described as an apocalypse, an end-of-the-world scenario. An invasion of the plague, of zombies, of bombs—of anything that could wipe out the entirety of all things living. Everything had been destroyed and they stood helpless.

The stench of death and isolation cloaked around them, and a shield of mist invaded inwards. They were the last to go, but soon they would learn that they had been defeated in their last attempt of survival. Everything had to be sacrificed, and it was their life that was the last to go. They had a few seconds to soak it all in beforehand; their lives literally flashing before their eyes, holding onto each other's hands for comfort. A solitary tear was the last thing to ever taint the world. They could feel the cold pouring into their soul; freezing their hearts and taking them to join him, to join what was seen to be the only thing resembling existence.

As their minds closed down, the world was forgotten and a new force was created.

Death.

Everything that is created must die, eventually.

This was the beginning of eternity. After life, all you have is Death. Death takes over and it becomes all you know. It taints everything. This is forever and it is the concept of forever that Death longs to be in control of.

This is how the New World was created. It was not like Heaven, nor did it resemble Hell—a place that everyone, including Death, feared. He stood on the edge of a mountain, watching as his essence penetrated anything that had survived the war between humanity. He understood how cold he seemed. He saw the light leave everything and he felt the sadness up until it's very last moment. He was most accustomed to it, so he understood the initial fear and loss of hope. He had tried to find a way to wipe out the fear but nothing ever worked. Death was never accepted.

Death was not evil. He was merciful, and he had grown tired of hearing the cries of the living. He had grown tired of watching the self-destruction that took place daily. He had offered comfort to those who were tired of living—but even still, the thought of Death tortured everybody else. Despite this, he welcomed his new family members every second of the day, working around the clock to rescue those who had fallen into his path.

As he picked them up with his cloak of darkness, he longed to offer comfort—but still he was surrounded by suffering. The world below him was never a happy world. For all of Earth's existence, he had watched this and was tormented by the repetitive nature of the living. He decided that he would need to save the world. He would give them the only comfort he was able to. An apocalypse is the right term, he felt. Although he didn't approve of the fear attached to this thought. He believed that this would save everyone; it would end unhappiness and create a new beginning.

He watched as his family grew ever bigger, as he became stronger. It was a cold place, but peaceful. As the final few joined him, he saw a look in their eyes. It was a longing sadness, but this soon faded. He watched as their eyes faded out and was overcome with the closest thing to contentment he had felt. He could no longer sense their pain or their anguish. It was something they would never have to experience again; they could live alongside each other knowing they would not ever lose one another.

Evelyn Knightley was born in Oxford, 1992.

After falling in love with the power of words and creative writing at a very young age, and during a time in which two very different paths in life presented themselves, she made the less than conventional choice of leaving the world of higher education in order to stay true to her inner child. Waving goodbye to the prospect of a Psychology degree, she is now giving the life of a broke writer a try.

This is a journey she welcomes you to join her on.

DISCONNECTED

A boat gently nudged against the shore, rhythmically mimicking the movement of the ocean beneath it. The waves licked the damaged oars that had been carelessly left hanging over the rim of the aged, and somewhat neglected, boat. The sun had fallen behind the edge of the ocean many hours ago, and in its place, a dark blanket veiled over the sky. The air was still and the surrounding land gave no signs that life could be found within its body. The only hint of an outside world came from the faint glow of the stars far off in the distance; any source of light had been scared away by motionless clouds that lay above the vastness of trees and mountains. It was like another world, they said, a place so disconnected from reality—yet more aware of the essence of life than they had ever known. That is why they searched for it, or so they say. They were not in search of a better life, nor a richer one—they were simply searching for a life that they could claim as their own.

I found their story in bits and pieces, scattered in secret places. There's a lot of it I don't understand, and I think it's because I've never been there. I can only imagine the things they describe and the lives they had lived for such a short while. I think I've found myself obsessed with their story, in the same way they became obsessed with creating it, and perhaps I should not share this with you in case you grow the same obsession. Whilst I accept that I alone cannot create my own story, I know I can share theirs, and I hope you know that is my only intention—to tell a story. You are already creating your own.

The Journey

They had found each other through one way or another: a support group, a quiet bar, a busy coffee shop, through mutual friends, in a class at college. It didn't matter how they met, not to them. Everything that happened in the past days held no significance. It was the journey they cared about. They breathed for it, and very quickly with no explanation, it became their meaning in life. I've tried explaining this to people, what I mean when I say 'the meaning of life,' but it's probably the only thing in life that can't be explained. I believe it's different for each individual. It changes as we age, as our hearts get broken and we learn how to love and how to deal with loss. This wasn't the case for them, or perhaps it had been at one point, but through their various ways they all developed the same meaning. It had been laid out in print, slipped into their favourite book or song; it became imprinted in their daily language. Their meaning of life became very simple, very impossible.

This is not your life. You must search for the life that belongs to you. Everything else is irrelevant. Search for your life.

They took it upon themselves to find a place where they would be the only thing that mattered. Everyday material objects would become irrelevant: the daily routine of a nine-to-five job, a work out at the gym, counting the units in each glass of wine—it would all be forgotten. All they needed was another like-minded person to assist them in their endeavour. They realised that for the time being, they still had one foot placed in the world they longed to leave behind. They realised that perhaps they weren't the only ones who had the desire to erase and recreate their own life. While they still had the means to reach out to others, an online forum was created. Just one on a free website and it never had any more than ten registered users. That was all they needed. They could combine their life skills in order to make their journey as easy as possible, and it was agreed that as soon as they arrived at their destination, it would be a solitary lifestyle. They were to use each other for the sake of convenience, but they were never allowed to lose sight of their goal, of the reasoning behind their efforts. A destination had been decided on. Although, it was claimed by all that it hadn't been a decision but more of a 'calling'. Each person claimed that they all knew of their destination without ever speaking of it, without ever planning it. It was a place that had summoned them and they answered in the obedient manner it demanded.

It took some time before I was able to fully comprehend the extent of the struggles they faced during their travel. It was a journey I failed to complete, and the secret to their success is something I'll never quite know. I can only assume that it was because I went in search of this place for curiosities sake, and not for the purpose of faith. My path was blocked long before I could even set my eyes on the shore, before I could really experience the darkness and sanctity that I have since learnt of. I can only speak of the vague descriptions they left in their place, so that will have to be enough.

They boarded a plane, flight number VX3501, London Heathrow to Indian Mountains, Utopia Creek, Alaska. From there they headed north, mostly by foot, occasionally by hitchhiking. With no true destination, it was easy enough for them to navigate to the edge of the land. Along the way, their group decreased in size; some blaming the never ending cold wind, others feigning illness. In the end, six people stood along the harbour, watching the sun rise for the last time, lost in their thoughts of the world they were leaving behind and consumed by anxiety. It was the strongest silence they had experienced, with their mind at full volume while the world around them disappeared into the background. They abandoned their backpacks on the land, rented a boat with their last bit of money—all promising the harbour guard that he would have full access to the entirety of their funds as they informed him that they had no intention of returning the boat. They opted for the smallest boat, an old wooden one that had been on many fishing trips; a boat that was capable of sailing far enough to the quietest part of the lakes, suitable for some offshore sightseeing in the calm weather—small enough to slip off the earth, unheard and unnoticed.

  As they stepped into the boat, knees touching, sharing body heat as the wind picked up and the sun became more prominent in the sky above them. He picked up the oars and began to push the boat out to the sea. Nobody looked back at the land they were leaving far behind. Nobody spoke. Nobody shed a tear. They could not remember how they came to be sat together, abandoning their lives, sharing a journey with strangers. They did not share stories, because they left them behind with their backpacks. All of their memories had been stuffed deep inside and abandoned in a place they had no intention of visiting in order to travel to a place they did not know of. He felt as though he was leading them, yet he knew he was no leader. Penniless and without possessions, they only had themselves for company. They lost themselves in a state of meditation, only occasionally emptying their minds of their thoughts when it became their turn to fill in a page of a notebook. The only item they had agreed to bring with them from their own world: a two-hundred page, thin-ruled notebook and two pens. They had not been touched until the boat had been boarded and their new lives were ready to begin. He started writing their story first, unsure of what to include, yet certain that the purging of his mind would allow him to be reborn. The notebook remained blank for what he thought had been two days. It presented itself as temptation to become a link to the world they had left in the distance. Still, it had its uses and they knew it was a temptation they had to overcome before opening up to the new life. No one knew how long the journey would be, but each of them fought with their inner demons to rid themselves of the past world—the older years.

2003 BA

The sky hasn't changed for what feels like days. I lost sight of the sun long ago. I don't know anybody else's name. I feel alone, and this time it's very real. I don't know what I expected from this journey. I guess maybe I just wanted to test myself; to see if I could really do it, just up and leave. I've left everyone behind, all my responsibilities, all the things I never wanted but now I think I've taken it all for granted. This has all become incredibly real very quickly. Everybody keeps looking at me as if I have the answers to their unspoken questions. They keep looking at me with need in their eyes. It's too late for me to turn back. I can't even remember how I ended up here, but I'm sure it can't have been that long ago since I decided to say my quiet goodbye to home. I suppose I shouldn't call it home; I'm heading towards a new home. I don't know why. If I'm honest, my head feels pretty empty right now. I keep trying to remember their faces, but the longer I spend in the middle of nothingness, the more my mind becomes filled with just that. Nothingness. Everything is becoming erased, and I think at one point that's what I wanted. But now it scares me. I don't know why I'm here or what I'm searching for. I don't know what pushed me this close to the edge, close enough to forget everyone and everything. Whatever it was, it's succeeding. The closer I get to... wherever it is, it becomes more real. I can see it in my mind now. Cars, mobile phones, coffee shops—it feels like they're just words I have made up. That isn't real anymore. Real is the shore. I can see it— the pale sand running into the stillness of the ocean and the trees towering over me. I can see it all. I keep telling myself that I'm sailing us to a place that's not so different to the world I know, but I stopped sailing a long time to go. I haven't touched the oar since land left my sight. The subtle movement of the waves have been moving us closer to the shore of our unknown land. I can already sense the difference in the air. It doesn't move but I can still feel the touch of nature on my cheeks. I'm no longer cold but I'm still shivering. The water looks different; it looks cleaner. Every so often I test the temperature and it feels like thick oil against my skin. I taste it and the further we've travelled, the less salt there seems to be. It keeps us dehydrated. It's like it's protecting us. There is no wind so the waves are gentle, the motion never changes. It seems to be swaying us like a lullaby. It never picks the boat up too high; we feel no threat of capsizing.

I've lost all sense of direction. Even as I'm writing this, I can feel it all changing. Not the world around me. I feel like I'm not in the world anymore, the ocean has taken us elsewhere. The sky isn't changing, nor the water or the wind. My mind is changing. I've been trying to hold on to the colour of her eyes and the scent of her skin, but even she is slipping away from me. I didn't tell her I was leaving, but I think she knew I was. I don't know why I think this, but I started to grow distant even when I was still with her. When she was shouting and crying at me, the blue of her eyes growing darker as I ignored her words. She turned her back on me on our last night, and I didn't say goodbye when I left the next morning. I knew I had hurt her, but she couldn't understand that I was doing it for both of us. I had my demons pulling me back, stopping me from loving her the way she deserved. I knew I had to go. Completely. She would never forgive me. Otherwise, I'd have pulled her down with me.

But now there's no fear of that because I can't remember her face. I once had every part of her mesmerised, but it's all slipping away from me, and I think the same is happening to her. She won't be able to remember my name by now, and I can't remember hers.

I suppose this is why I'm here, on this boat, in some ocean. Latitude and Longitude mean nothing to me now that I'm here. I know I have left and I know something greater is waiting for me. I've done this for her. For them. I would have pulled all of them down.

Cal.

SOUNDTRACK

I couldn't have finished this book without the help of music keeping me company throughout many sleepless nights. These are a few (of the many) songs that I owe thanks to.

Alexisonfire- Born and Raised
Biffy Clyro- Machines
City and Colour- Happiness by the Kilowatt
CoMa & Owsey- Imagine That
Daughter- Youth
Evanescence- Disappear
Fiona Apple- Sleep to Dream
The Glass Child- Somewhere I Belong
Kodaline- High Hopes
Lykke Li- Little Bit
Marilyn Manson- Coma Black: Eden/ The Apple of Discord
Owsey- Places We Never Went Together
Paramore- Last Hope
Tori Amos- Taxi Ride

www.ingramcontent.com/pod-product-compliance
Lightning Source LLC
Chambersburg PA
CBHW060712030426
42337CB00017B/2845